Tiburones/Sharks

Tiburón martillo/ Hammerhead Shark

por/by Deborah Nuzzolo

Editor Consultor/Consulting Editor: Dra. Gail Saunders-Smith

Consultor/Consultant: Jody Rake, member
Southwest Marine/Aquatic Educators' Association

CAPSTONE PRESS
a capstone imprint

Pebble Plus is published by Capstone Press,
151 Good Counsel Drive, P.O. Box 669, Mankato, Minnesota 56002.
www.capstonepress.com

092009
005618CGS10

 Books published by Capstone Press are manufactured with
paper containing at least 10 percent post-consumer waste.

Library of Congress Cataloging-in-Publication Data
Nuzzolo, Deborah.
    [Hammerhead shark. Spanish & English]
    Tiburón martillo = Hammerhead shark / por/by Deborah Nuzzolo.
    p. cm. — (Pebble plus bilingüe/bilingual. Tiburones/sharks)
    Includes index.
    Summary: "Simple text and photographs present hammerhead sharks, their body parts, and their
behavior — in both English and Spanish" — Provided by publisher.
    ISBN 978-1-4296-4802-8 (library binding)
    1. Hammerhead sharks — Juvenile literature. I. Title. II. Title: Hammerhead shark. III. Series.
QL638.95.S7N8918 2010
597.3'4 — dc22   2009037866

Editorial Credits
Megan Peterson, editor; Strictly Spanish, translation services; Katy Kudela, bilingual editor;
    Ted Williams, set designer; Kyle Grenz, book designer; Jo Miller, photo researcher;
    Eric Manske and Danielle Ceminsky, production specialists

Photo Credits
Alamy/Danita Delimont, 19
BigStockPhoto.com/phred, 1
Bruce Coleman Inc./Ron & Valerie Taylor, cover
Dreamstime/Katseyephoto, 16–17
Getty Images Inc./Iconica/Jeff Rotman, 9; National Geographic/Brian Skerry, 20–21
Nature Picture Library/Doug Perrine, 10–11
Peter Arnold/BIOS Bios - Auteurs (droits geres) Cole Brandon, 15; Jeffery L. Rotman, 13; Jonathan Bird, 7
Shutterstock/Simone Conti, backgrounds
Tom Stack & Associates, Inc./Dave Fleetham, 4–5

Note to Parents and Teachers

The Tiburones/Sharks set supports national science standards related to the
characteristics and behavior of animals. This book describes and illustrates hammerhead
sharks in both English and Spanish. The images support early readers in understanding
the text. The repetition of words and phrases helps early readers learn new words. This
book also introduces early readers to subject-specific vocabulary words, which are
defined in the Glossary section. Early readers may need assistance to read some words
and to use the Table of Contents, Internet Sites, and Index sections of the book.

Table of Contents

Tabla de contenidos

Hammer for a Head

Can you guess how the hammerhead shark got its name? Its wide head looks like the top of a hammer.

Un martillo por cabeza

¿Puedes adivinar cómo obtuvo su nombre el tiburón martillo? Su cabeza ancha se parece a la parte superior de un martillo.

Hammerhead sharks live in warm, shallow seas. They swim alone or in groups called schools.

Los tiburones martillo viven en mares de aguas templadas y poco profundas. Ellos nadan solos o en grupos llamados escuelas.

A Hammerhead's Life

Hammerhead shark pups are

born live. Between six and

42 pups are born at one time.

La vida de un tiburón martillo

Las crías de un tiburón martillo

nacen vivas. Entre seis y 42

crías nacen al mismo tiempo.

Nine kinds of hammerheads swim
in the sea. Bonnetheads are the smallest.
Great hammerheads are the largest.

Nueve tipos de tiburón martillo nadan
en el mar. Los tiburones cabeza
de pala son los más pequeños.
El gran tiburón martillo
es el más grande.

bonnethead/cabeza de pala
5 feet (1.5 meters) long/
5 pies (1.5 metros) de largo

**great hammerhead/
gran tiburón martillo**
15 feet (4.6 meters) long/
15 pies (4.6 metros) de largo

5 feet (1.5 meters) long/
5 pies (1.5 metros) de largo

bonnethead/
cabeza de pala

What They Look Like

Hammerheads have an eye

on each side of their wide head.

They can spot prey easily.

A qué se parecen

Los tiburones martillo tienen un ojo

en cada lado de su cabeza ancha.

Ellos pueden ubicar a su presa fácilmente.

13

Hammerhead sharks have two
dorsal fins on their back.
Dorsal fins help sharks keep
their balance while swimming.

Los tiburones martillo tienen dos aletas
dorsales en su espalda. Las aletas
dorsales ayudan a los tiburones a
mantener el equilibrio mientras nadan.

**dorsal fins/
aletas dorsales**

15

Hunting

Hammerhead sharks hunt fish, stingrays, and other sharks. They eat crabs and squid too.

Caza

Los tiburones martillo cazan peces, rayas y otros tiburones. También comen cangrejos y calamares.

Hammerheads often hunt
on the ocean floor.
They look for stingrays
hidden in the sand.

Los tiburones martillo cazan
frecuentemente en el suelo
del océano. Ellos buscan
rayas escondidas en la arena.

Hammerhead sharks
can find prey anywhere.
It's not easy to hide
from these amazing hunters.

Los tiburones martillo pueden
encontrar presas en cualquier
lugar. No es fácil esconderse
de estos magníficos cazadores.

Glossary

balance — steadiness; sharks use their fins to stay balanced while swimming in the water.

fin — a body part that fish use to swim and steer in water

hunt — to chase and kill animals for food

prey — an animal hunted by another animal for food

pup — a young shark

school — a group of fish; as many as 100 hammerhead sharks might gather in a school.

Internet Sites

FactHound offers a safe, fun way to find Internet sites related to this book. All of the sites on FactHound have been researched by our staff.

Here's all you do:

Visit *www.facthound.com*

FactHound will fetch the best sites for you!

Glosario

la aleta — una parte del cuerpo de un pez usada para nadar y guiar en el agua

cazar — perseguir y matar animales para comer

la cría — un tiburón joven

el equilibrio — firmeza; los tiburones usan sus aletas para mantener el equilibrio cuando nadan en el agua.

la escuela — un grupo de peces; hasta 100 tiburones martillo pueden juntarse en una escuela.

la presa — un animal cazado por otro para comérselo

Sitios de Internet

FactHound brinda una forma segura y divertida de encontrar sitios de Internet relacionados con este libro. Todos los sitios en FactHound han sido investigados por nuestro personal.

Esto es todo lo que tú necesitas hacer:

Visita *www.facthound.com*

¡FactHound buscará los mejores sitios para ti!

Index

Índice